EXPERT BLOGGER

EXPERT

BLOGGER

EXPERT BLOGGER

INDEX

Blog for everyone?

Learning about Blogging

Maintaining a successful blog

Manage multiple blogs

Supervising your child's blog

Optimizing your blog for search engines

Ordering when you buy online

Products to facilitate blogs

Promoting your blog

Tips to keep your blog up to date

Use of guest bloggers

When others don't approve of your blog

What is a Blogger?

A Blogger is a person - or a group of people - who manages a site or social network on the Internet with the aim of entertaining, informing or selling.

It is the Blogger who maintains direct contact with the public and communicates with his or her visitors directly.

A Blogger can devote himself or herself to publishing interesting content for the specific audience of his or her blog, in addition to promoting products or services.

Therefore, a Blogger is a person who can (or cannot) engage in Digital Marketing or Content Marketing.

Affiliate Marketing and Blogging

Affiliate marketing is a way for bloggers to use their blog to generate revenue. The amount of revenue generated by a blog with affiliate marketing links can vary significantly depending on the amount of traffic the blog receives, as well as the compensation offered by the affiliate marketing. Affiliate marketing essentially involves creating a link on your blog to another company's website. The other company then compensates the owner of the blog according to a previously agreed contract. This compensation can be granted in several different ways. The blog owner can be compensated each time the ad is

9

published, each time a unique visitor to the website clicks on the ad, or each time a blog visitor performs a desired action, such as making a purchase or registering on the website. This article will discuss some aspects of affiliate marketing that bloggers should understand, including selecting opportunities carefully, maximizing the revenue potential for these opportunities, and understanding the requirements associated with these affiliate marketing opportunities.

Selecting Affiliate Marketing Opportunities

There are a variety of affiliate marketing opportunities available. Many different companies and websites offer affiliate marketing opportunities. In most cases, the blog owner simply needs to submit their blog website address along with some other basic

information for approval. In most cases, the company is unlikely to reject the application unless the website content is deemed objectionable or in conflict with the company's objectives. However, while getting approval to display affiliate links on your website is a fairly simple process, this does not mean that blog owners should select these affiliate marketing opportunities without discretion. It is a much better idea to carefully select affiliate marketing opportunities with companies that are of interest to the blog's target audience.

A well-focused blog that is reaching a specific target audience should try to display marketing links that direct website traffic to companies that complement the blog without acting as a direct competitor to the blog. This helps ensure that blog visitors are not only interested in the affiliate marketing links and

therefore more likely to click on the links, but will also help ensure that blog visitors do not find the affiliate marketing links annoying.

Maximizing Affiliate Marketing Opportunities

Once blog owners have selected affiliate marketing opportunities, it's time to consider how they can maximize the profits generated by these links. There are a couple of critical factors that blog owners should consider carefully to help maximize their affiliate marketing profits. This includes regularly evaluating the effectiveness of affiliate links and promoting the blog to maximize traffic.

Blog owners who incorporate affiliate marketing into their blog should regularly

evaluate the effectiveness of the affiliate links. This can be done by comparing the percentage of blog visitors who click on affiliate links to overall blog traffic. A blog that has a lot of traffic but a relatively small percentage of visitors clicking on the affiliate links should consider making changes to try to attract more blog visitors to click on the links. These changes may involve the aesthetics, size, or location of the ads. Making only one change at a time is recommended because it makes it easier for the blog owner to evaluate which changes are most beneficial. Blog owners can also help maximize profits from their affiliate marketing opportunities by doing self-promotion to boost an additional website to the blog. This is likely to be beneficial because increased website traffic will generally translate into higher affiliate marketing profits. In addition, the blog owner may occasionally mention companies

that they are affiliated with to generate interest in the website's ads.

Understanding Affiliate Marketing Requirements

Finally, blog owners should pay special attention to the affiliate marketing agreements they sign. This is important because some companies may impose restrictions on the use of a link to their website. This may include restrictions such as avoiding objectionable content, not including links or ads for direct competitors, or restrictions on the appearance of affiliate links. Failure to comply with these guidelines may result in the blog losing affiliate privileges and the blog owner being denied compensation.

Blogging for fun

Although blogs can be used for a variety of other purposes, such as generating income, promoting a cause, and providing information, there are many bloggers who enjoy blogging simply because it's fun. These bloggers enjoy blogging for reasons such as keeping in touch with friends, expressing themselves, or keeping track of important events. This article will explain how blogs can be used for these purposes.

Blogging to keep in touch with friends

Keeping in touch with friends and family is just one of the many reasons a person may

want to start a blog. This is especially useful for those who are away from their friends and family. Keeping in touch by phone, regular visits and even email are not always easy. This is because it can be difficult to maintain long-distance interactions with several different people at once. However, by maintaining a blog, one person can greatly simplify the process of keeping in touch with friends and family because they don't have to repeat information in individual phone calls or emails or make time to visit several different people.

By maintaining a blog, the individual can choose to post a variety of information and photos. Through this information and photos, the blog owner can keep others informed about current events in his or her life. Friends and family can view the blog at their convenience to catch up on important

events in the blog owner's life and, in most cases, can post comments to the blog owner. They can also read comments from others. This is beneficial if those who view the blog know each other because not only can they keep in touch with the blog owner, but they also have the opportunity to communicate with other friends and family through the blog's comment section.

Blogging as a form of expression

Some bloggers start blogging as a form of expression. They may edit poetry, songs, stories, or even use the blog to vent about personal or political events. These bloggers may wish to keep their blog private or they may make the blog available to the public. Keeping your blog private is a bit like keeping a diary or journal. It gives the

blogger a multimedia way to express themselves without the risk of others discovering their true feelings, innermost dreams, or frustrations. Other bloggers choose to make these blogs public. This can be for several different reasons. Sharing these feelings with others allows the blogger to reach out to others who may have the same interest as the blogger.

Bloggers who use their blog as a form of self-expression may want to be cautious and consider the decision to make a blog public. This is important because the owner of the blog may not initially see a problem in allowing others to see his or her personal thoughts. However, over time they may realize that their blog could be offensive to others or could cause problems if friends or family see it.

Blogging to keep track of events

Another common reason for blogging is to keep track of important events. Examples of some types of events a blogger may want to document include a pregnancy, wedding, vacation, sporting event, or the completion of school events. Using blogs to keep track of these events gives the blogger the opportunity to record daily events in a simple location where they can easily look back on the blog or share the posts with others who may be interested in the events. In these cases, the blog can serve as a form of a scrapbook that documents events as they occur. The blog owner can post as many times as they wish and can choose to include items such as photos, music, audio and video files in the blog. The blog can also be

designed to accommodate the events being documented. For example, a journal that represents a vacation may have backgrounds, fonts, and colors that represent the vacation location, while a pregnancy blog may feature elements that represent pregnancy, babies, and parenting.

Blogging for profit

Blogs are becoming an increasingly popular way for entrepreneurs to make a living online while doing something they really enjoy. In many cases, bloggers can make a profit with very little effort. There may be some work involved at first with designing a method to earn income and promote the website, but once this is established, simply maintaining the blog with periodicals may be enough to maintain the income. Two of the most popular methods for generating a profit from blogs include advertising methods. This includes advertising with AdSense and securing independent advertisers. This article will discuss these two methods of advertising on a blog.

21

Using AdSense to generate revenue

Using AdSense is one of the most popular ways for bloggers to generate income from their blog. This method is very popular because it is also very simple. AdSense is a program offered by Google where bloggers agree to have ads on their website and are compensated when users click on these ads. Bloggers simply have to create a blog and submit the address of the blog's website as well as other information to apply for participation in AdSense. Once a blog is approved, the owner receives a code that they can simply copy and paste to display ads on their blog. Google then posts appropriate ads each time the blog is accessed. Whenever possible, ads posted on the blog are closely related to the content of

the blog because Google crawls the website in advance to determine which ads are relevant to the content. Blog owners have some ability to impose restrictions on the types of ads that can appear on the blog. For example, the blog owner can specify that adult ads will not appear on the blog and Google will filter them.

How advertising revenue on a blog generates revenue

Many bloggers use ads on their blogs to generate revenue. This method of advertising is more difficult than using AdSense, but can be significantly more beneficial financially for the blogger. This method of advertising is similar to the type of targeted advertising often seen in magazines. For example, parenting magazines often feature ads that

will appeal to parents, such as ads for toys, children's clothing, or foods popular with children. Similarly, a running magazine may feature ads for shoes, sportswear, racing or training equipment. In these cases, advertisers pay for advertising space in the magazine in the hope that the magazine's audience will be attracted to buy products or services after seeing these ads.

Blog owners may use this type of advertising, but it can be difficult to find willing advertisers. However, there are some factors that may make an advertiser more willing to have an ad appear on a blog. One of the most important factors for advertisers is the amount of traffic the blog receives. This is important because advertisers who pay for advertising space are more likely to invest in a blog with a lot of traffic than one with very little traffic.

Another important factor for advertisers is the focus of the blog. Advertisers are more likely to buy advertising space from a blog with a specific focus of interest to the advertiser's target audience. Like the examples listed above from parent and runner magazines, advertisers want to advertise on a blog that is already reaching the same target audience.

Bloggers who use advertising on their website can be compensated in different ways. Some advertisers may pay a flat fee to have the ad published on the website for a certain period of time or for a certain number of page views. This means that the advertiser can buy space for a certain number of days, weeks or months or can buy space for a certain number of times the ad is served to

the website visitors.

Alternatively, the advertiser can choose to compensate the blogger according to the number of times specific actions occur. This may include users clicking on the ad or making a purchase after clicking on the ad. The type of compensation offered will need to be worked out in advance between the blogger and the advertiser to determine a fair payment method.

Blogging on a social network

Blogs are becoming increasingly popular and social networks are also becoming more popular. Social networks include popular websites such as MySpace.com where users can create personal websites and interact with other users. These websites can include a wide range of components including text, images, audio, video and blogs. Here users of the system can express their opinions, provide updates on their life, offer information on current events or fulfill a number of other objectives. However, bloggers who use a social network to maintain their blog must consider some different factors. This article will discuss

27

some of these factors, including whether blogs are available to the public or whether they are kept private, considering the blog's audience and dealing with harassment through the blog.

Making Blogs Private or Public

Most social networks allow users to make their website private or public. Private Websites are only available to the user and other users you specifically approve to view your website, while public websites are available to all users of the system. These same capabilities also apply to blogs that are maintained on a social network. For this reason, bloggers must determine whether or not they want their blog posts to be available to the entire social network or only to a fraction of this network.

This decision will be based largely on a matter of personal preference. Social networks can be quite extensive, and some bloggers may fear that their blog will be available to such a large audience, while other bloggers may not have apprehensions about the size of the potential audience. Bloggers should carefully consider this option before looking at a blog, but always have the option of changing this setting after the blog has been established if they change their mind about the choice they originally made.

Considering the blog's audience

Bloggers who use a social network to maintain a blog should also carefully

consider the potential audience for the blog. Most social networks include a broad cross-section of the general public. Therefore, bloggers should take this audience into account when posting a blog and should consider how members of the public will interpret the blog entries. While it will never be possible to avoid offending all potential audience members, some bloggers may consider at least trying to ensure that the blog posts they post are appropriate for all members of the social network. If this is not possible, the blogger may consider making the blog private.

Dealing with bullying through the blog

Another aspect that bloggers using a social network to publish their blog should be aware of is the potential for harassment of

other members through the blog. This may be in the form of offensive comments posted in response to blog entries. Depending on the degree of harassment, the blogger may choose to ignore these comments or take stronger action. Bloggers should review the social network's policies and seek their help in dealing with harassment from other users. In most cases, dealing with the problem can be as simple as blocking the user from commenting on the blog, but in some cases it may be necessary to contact social network administrators to try to get the user kicked off the system. In this situation, the administrators will review the situation and decide whether or not the user has violated the terms of service.

Blog software

With blogs becoming increasingly popular, there is also a growing need for software to simplify the blogging process. However, there are many different software packages available that can make the selection of a package seem overwhelming. However, selecting a software package doesn't have to be difficult. Bloggers can find websites that provide comparison charts for different software packages for simply the decision making process. These charts can save the blogger a great deal of time and effort because they gather a great deal of information in one convenient location. The blogger may still need additional information before using these comparison charts to make a decision. The article will provide

information about some of this additional information that may be useful, such as how to understand the comparison charts, methods for comparing software packages, and tips for selecting a blog software package.

Blogging Software Criteria

Those interested in starting or maintaining a blog should fully understand the blog software criteria before attempting to compare software packages. Some of the criteria that are important to understand include minimum server, data storage, and post editor requirements. Understanding these criteria is critical to the process of comparing and selecting blog software packages.

The minimum server requirements refer to the minimum requirements for the server on which the software will be installed. In most cases, the power and speed of the server is not relevant, but rather depends on the power and speed of the software required for the blog software to function properly. There may be additional costs associated with this software, as well as additional licensing requirements.

Data storage is also an important part of the evaluation of blog software packages. This may include options such as a flat file, data file or database. A flat file refers to storage options where the entire page is extracted each time a browser requests the blog. A data file refers to situations where the blog data is inserted into a template when a browser requests the blog. A database refers to storage options where the required

information is extracted from a flat file and inserted into a template when a browser requests the blog.

The publisher of posts is another criterion that a blogger may want to investigate carefully before selecting blog software. The post editor refers to the type of editor that will be used to complete the posts listed on the blog. These input methods can include options such as HTML or JAVA.

Comparison of blogging software packages

Bloggers looking for a blog software package should carefully compare the different software packages available. This is important because obviously some software packages are superior to others. It is also

important because some software packages may be more suited to the needs of a particular blog than other packages. When comparing blog software packages, it is important that the blogger first carefully considers the needs of the blog. This is important because it will help the blogger realize which criteria are most relevant to his or her particular blog.

Selecting Blogging Software Packages

After carefully evaluating the blog software packages, it is time for the blogger to make a decision and select one of the available packages. Ideally, the blogger will already have compared important data such as storage space, server requirements and post editors. However, the blogger should also consider other factors such as cost and

versatility. Many blogging software packages are available for free, while there are some that are available for purchase. The blogger will have to decide whether a software package is worth buying or not, or whether free software packages will meet his or her blogging needs.

After considering the criteria and cost of the software, the blogger should consider viewing sample blogs created with a particular software package. This is a good idea because these samples can provide a good indication of the software's capabilities. This is because, in general, the higher the quality of the samples, the greater the capabilities of the software.

Blogging to promote a cause

While many bloggers maintain a blog for personal or social reasons or to generate income, there are other bloggers who use their blogs to promote a cause. These blogs may be targeted to a specific political or social cause, depending on the blogger's interests, as well as the blogger's view that the blog can bring about the political or social changes he or she is seeking. Blogs that are committed to promoting a particular cause may face more adversity than blogs with a lighter theme, but they can also be very effective. However, blog owners who choose to maintain this type of blog should be aware of the ramifications of this type of blog. For

example, blog owners may receive negative comments from blog readers who disagree with the cause. This article will offer some tips on choosing a cause for a blog and promoting the blog to interested visitors.

Choosing a Cause for a Blog

Choosing a cause for a blog can vary in difficulty from extremely easy to incredibly difficult. The difficulty of making this decision will depend largely on the personal beliefs of the blog owner. A blog owner who is already committed to a particular cause will probably find this decision to be fairly simple, while blog owners who do not have strong social or political convictions or who have a wide variety of causes they wish to promote may find this decision to be quite difficult. However, there are some factors

that the blog owner should consider carefully before selecting a cause to promote on a blog.

First, the blog owner should select a topic for which they already have enough knowledge or are willing to do a lot of research. This is important because the blog owner must post blog entries on a regular basis. These blog entries must be accurate and informative to the reader. Therefore, the blog owner should be well versed in the topic or at least interested in learning more about it.

Blog owners should also carefully consider the potential to influence blog visitors with respect to the blog's topic. Although it will not be possible to convince all blog visitors to believe in the cause promoted by the blog, the blog owner should select a topic that he or she is sure will influence blog visitors to

agree with the views presented in the blog.

Promoting the blog to interested visitors

Once the blog owner decides on a theme for the blog, it's time to find out how to promote the blog to the target audience. This can be achieved in several different ways. For the sake of brevity, this article will discuss promoting a blog through search engine optimization and promoting a blog through participation in relevant forums.

Search engine optimization is a very effective way to promote a blog. This practice involves making efforts to increase search engine rankings to ensure that interested Internet users are directed to the blog. This can be done in a number of different ways,

including careful use of appropriate keywords, appropriate use of tags such as title tags and image tags, and generating back links to the blog. All of these efforts can help improve search engine rankings which should also improve blog traffic.

Blog owners can also promote their blog by participating in relevant forums and message boards. The blog owner can simply participate in these forums and provide relevant information while including a link to the blog in their signature. Other forum users are likely to click on the link if the blog owner is respected within the forum. The blog owner can even incorporate a link to their blog in the body of the forum posts if it is appropriate and acceptable according to the message board guidelines.

Blogging with Wordpress

Wordpress is one of the many options available to bloggers looking for free software online, making it incredibly easy to publish your own blog. This software is easy to use, provides a variety of templates, and offers excellent support for bloggers. There are many options available to bloggers and other blogging programs may be better known and offer slightly different features, but many bloggers are quite satisfied with Wordpress. This article will provide useful information for bloggers who are considering starting a blog with Wordpress, such as reasons to choose Wordpress, tips on starting a blog, and information on the support offered by Wordpress. Based on this information, as well as your own research

bloggers can decide if Wordpress is right for them or if they should look for a different blog network.

Reasons to choose Wordpress

There are many good reasons to choose Wordpress to start a blog. Some of these reasons include a wide variety of templates, the ability to easily categorize and tag posts, features such as spell checker, previews, and autosave, the ability to post text, audio and video files, a variety of privacy options, and the ability to track blog-related statistics, in addition to other great features. Some of these features may be more important to some bloggers than others, so deciding whether Wordpress is right for you will largely be a matter of personal preference. For example, bloggers with little or no

programming experience may enjoy the large number of templates available in Wordpress, while bloggers who are concerned about privacy issues may be more interested in the privacy options available through Wordpress. Carefully researching these features will help bloggers determine whether they should start a blog with Wordpress.

Starting a Blog with Wordpress

Bloggers who choose to start a blog with Wordpress certainly won't be disappointed by the amount of time it takes to start a blog. A blogger can literally start a blog with Wordpress in minutes. This is tremendously important for bloggers who are eager to get started and don't want to deal with the lengthy process of starting a blog. The only

requirements for starting a blog are a valid email address and a username. The blogger enters this information on the registration page and receives a password almost instantly. Then, the blogger simply has to check his or her email, follow the activation link provided, and use the password provided and the process is complete. The blogger can start blogging immediately.

Support offered by Wordpress

For many first-time bloggers, the type of support offered is very important. This is because first-time bloggers may have a lot of questions about the process of starting a basic blog and, once they establish a basic blog, they may have additional questions about using advanced features and customizing the blog. Wordpress offers a great deal of

support for bloggers of all levels. Support offered by Wordpress includes the ability to contact support staff, as well as the ability to receive support from other members through online forums. Although the support staff is incredibly responsive, some bloggers enjoy the ability to communicate with other bloggers in forums. This is because the forums are active 24 hours a day and bloggers can find support from their peers at any time.

Careers in Blogging

Many freelance writers are beginning to find that blogs are one of the newest career opportunities available to them. Blogging is essentially a series of publications on a particular topic that are listed in reverse chronological order. These blogs can be on a variety of different topics and can be personal, political, informational, humorous, or any other category desired by the blogger. However, the key to a successful blog is a blog that addresses a topic that appeals to a broad audience. In addition, the blog should be regularly updated and should provide useful content to the readers of the blog. This article will provide information on finding career opportunities in blogging, discuss the benefits of this type of career, and provide

48

information on how writers can successfully manage a blog.

Finding Career Opportunities in Blogging

Although career opportunities in blogging are becoming increasingly popular, many writers are not aware of how to find these wonderful opportunities. These career opportunities can be offered as ghost writing positions or as positions that offer a profile for the writer and finding these blog opportunities is often very similar to finding other career opportunities for writers. Companies looking for a blogger can post the job offer in the same way that they would post other vacancies in the company, such as accounting positions or administrative positions. Therefore, writers interested in a position as a blogger should use the same job

search websites they rely on to find other career opportunities.

Bloggers can also visit career websites and message boards that focus exclusively on career blogs. The ProBlogger.net website is just one example of a website dedicated exclusively to connecting bloggers with those who are interested in hiring a writer for a particular blog. Interested bloggers should also consider joining forums for those who blog for a living. This can be beneficial because bloggers here are likely to share information about the companies they work for, as well as any information they have about companies currently seeking to hire bloggers.

The benefits of a career in blogging

There are many benefits to pursuing a career in blogging. Perhaps one of the most attractive benefits to a career in blogging is that the work can usually be done as a telework position. This is because as long as the blogger has access to the software needed to write and upload a blog, it is not necessary for the blogger to do the work from a specific location. This means that the blogger can reside virtually anywhere in the world and can probably do the necessary work from home. However, not all blogging positions are teleworking positions. Some companies may require bloggers to perform work on site as a matter of personal preference.

Another benefit of a career in blogging is the ability to do the work at a pace that is

convenient for the blogger. The blogger may be required to upload a new blog post on a regular schedule, but actual writing of the posts can be accomplished when it is convenient for the blogger. Many blogging software packages allow the blogger to set a specific time for a specific post to be uploaded. This allows the blogger to write several posts at once and have them published according to a predetermined schedule.

Finding time to blog

One of the problems many bloggers face is finding the time to blog. This is especially difficult if the blogger maintains several blogs or if the blogger maintains a blog of current events where posts must be timely to be relevant and interesting to readers.

Writing blog posts in batches and scheduling them for posting as needed is one way to deal with managing multiple blogs. However, current event blog writers should take special care to budget their time wisely to ensure that they are posting current blog posts. One way to accomplish this is to set aside time each day to read current events for inspiration and then schedule time to write and post the blog. For example, a blogger with a current events blog might choose to review the previous day's news first thing in the morning to ensure that he or she is reviewing all relevant news from the previous day before writing the blog post.

Managing comments on your blog

Most blogs allow blog visitors to post comments on any of the blog posts. These comments can be from the blog post or they can be completely unrelated to the blog post. Comments can also be positive or negative in nature. Regardless of the type of comment left by a visitor, the blogger may choose to handle these comments in a number of different ways. The blogger can respond to these comments, prevent individual visitors from leaving comments in the future, or use administrative functions to remove comments or set up the blog to require approval of comments before they are posted on the blog. This article will discuss each of

54

these options for handling comments on a blog in more detail.

Responding to comments on your blog

Bloggers who receive comments on their blog may want to respond to these comments. Most blog programs allow the blogger to post comments on their own blog, allowing them to respond directly. With this feature, a blogger can deal with a number of different situations, including negative comments, positive comments, and questions. Bloggers who receive negative comments on their blog may choose to respond to these comments directly with a rebuttal to the negative comments. This allows the blogger to acknowledge the criticism and defend their original post. Bloggers who receive positive comments can also respond to these

comments to thank visitors for the praise. Even other bloggers may receive comments that ask a question about the blog post or about the blogger himself. Bloggers may choose to answer these questions to develop a better relationship with visitors to the blog.

Blocking Comments from Individual Visitors

Another option for dealing with blog comments that are negative in nature is to block comments from individual visitors to the blog. In most cases, bloggers will have the ability to blog a particular user so that they do not leave comments on the blog. The blogger may wish to use this option in situations where the blog visitor's comments are extremely mean. The blogger may also wish to prohibit individual visitors to the

blog from commenting if they have previously tried to explain their point to the visitor but the visitor continues to post negative comments. A blogger may also wish to prohibit an individual visitor from commenting if he or she believes that the comments are being left as spam.

Use administrative features

Another option for handling comments on a blog includes using administrative features to delete comments or changing the settings to not allow comments to be displayed until the blogger approves them. Blog owners often have the ability to delete a comment left by a visitor to the blog. Deleting these comments is usually a fairly simple process. However, it is not a completely effective method because other visitors to the blog

may have the opportunity to read these comments before they are deleted. Therefore, deleting the comment may prevent some visitors from reading it, but it will not guarantee that any visitor to the blog will see it. However, there is a way for bloggers to ensure that visitors do not read negative comments. Most types of blogging software have options that require the blogger to approve all comments before they are available to the public. This gives the blogger the ability to remove a comment before it is read by any of the visitors to the blog. The blogger can simply delete any comments that they do not want others to read before the comments are posted.

Design elements of a blog

A blog can essentially be an online diary that is displayed in reverse chronological order, but it is also a website that requires the same attention to detail as any other website. It also requires the same design elements as a normal website that also does not function as a blog. Bloggers have to make decisions regarding the design elements of the blog, such as colors and layout, fonts, and the inclusion of ads. Although many blog software programs provide a variety of templates that make designing a blog fairly simple, blogs can also be highly customized by bloggers who possess some programming skills. This article will discuss some of the basic design considerations that bloggers encounter.

Blog Colors and Layouts

The colors and design of a blog are one of the most obvious design considerations that bloggers should take into account when starting or redesigning their blog. Bloggers can use a solid color background, blocks of different colors on the background, or images or textures on the background. These background elements can be any color imaginable. However, bloggers who are considering colors for use in their blog should consider using colors that are aesthetically pleasing to most visitors to the blog. This is important because using bright colors that are hard on the eyes can reduce blog traffic.

The design of the blog should also be carefully considered by the blogger. The blog

should be organized in a way that is attractive to blog visitors, fits the blog's theme, and is presented in a logical way that is easy for visitors to follow. Again, this is important because if a design that meets these criteria is not used, blog visitors may choose not to visit the blog because the design is confusing or unattractive.

Sources used in a blog

Bloggers have a number of options available to them when selecting sources to use on their blog. These options include the font chosen, text size, and text color. Bloggers should consider choosing a font that works well with the overall blog layout and fits the blog's theme, but is also a common font. This is important because visitors to the blog may have trouble seeing the font if the blogger

selects a unique font that is not common. Text size and text colors should also be carefully considered. These elements are mainly important for readability. The text size should be set so that members of the target audience can read the text easily. For example, a blogger with older people as a target audience may choose to use a slightly larger text size than usual. The colours used for the text should also be selected to improve readability. One way to do this is to select colours that are attractive to the eye but also contrast with the background colour.

Including advertisements in a blog

Bloggers should also consider including ads when designing their blogs. This includes determining whether or not to include blogs. Once this decision is made, bloggers who

choose to include ads should carefully consider how and where they want to display these ads. Ads can be displayed in various locations throughout the blog and can be designed to be discreet or obvious, depending on the blogger's preferences. Ads can also come in a variety of sizes and shapes and are highly customizable in different ways.

Find blogs to read

There are a variety of blogs available today. Internet users are lucky enough to have a large number of blogs to choose from when looking for a blog to read regularly. There are also often many blogs available that cover a particular topic. Blogs can be about any topic imaginable. Some blogs are created to entertain, while others are created to inform. Some blogs are created to generate profit, while others are created to help others. With so many blogs currently available online, it can be difficult to determine which blogs are worth reading and which are not. It can also be difficult to limit the number of blogs a web user reads. This article will provide information on how to find and select blogs to read, including using search engines to

find blogs, finding blogs by participating in message boards, and finding recommendations for blogs from friends or family.

Using search engines to find blogs

Search engines are one of the most trusted resources Internet users often rely on to find useful websites. However, it is important to note that search engines can also be extremely useful for Internet users who are interested in finding blogs to read. An Internet user who is looking for a blog on a particular topic can begin the process of finding these blogs by entering relevant keywords or phrases into a popular search engine and carefully reviewing the results provided for this search. However, this type of search will not necessarily provide Internet

users with blogs. In fact, the search results may not include a blog on any of the first pages in the search results despite returning pages and pages of links to useful websites. An easy way for the Internet user to use search engines to find blogs related to a particular topic is to include the word blog with the keywords or phrases entered in the search engine. This will help filter the search results and can push blogs to the front of the search results. However, it is best for Internet users to search for blog collections and then look within these collections for those of interest.

Finding blogs on message boards

Many Internet users rely on message boards to find interesting and informative blogs. This is because many message board

participants who have a blog often find ways to let others know about the blog. This can be through the process of incorporating a link to the blog in the user's signature on the message board or, when appropriate, providing the link to the blog directly in the body of a message in the message board. Although many bloggers can take advantage of the opportunity to promote their own blog through message boards, those who are interested in finding new blogs will probably not have time to review all of these blogs. Therefore, it is advisable that these Internet users discriminate a little bit about the blogs they choose to visit. One way to do this is to visit only regular forum board blogs that offer valuable information for message board conversations. The Internet user can also avoid blogs that appear to be posted as spam. This is important because not only are these blogs likely to be of poor quality, but visiting these blogs encourages the blog owner to

continue spamming with their link.

Looking for blog recommendations

Finally, Internet users looking for blogs to read regularly may consider seeking recommendations from friends or family who share a particular interest. Friends or family who are interested in the same topic as you can already read blogs relevant to this interest on a regular basis. It's worth asking them for recommendations because they have no reason to do anything other than recommend blogs that they really enjoy and assume that you will be interested as well. In addition, this method of finding blogs is ideal because your friends and family are likely to be well aware of your tastes and expectations and will guide you in the right direction.

Find your niche blog

Finding your blogging niche should be one of the aspects of blogging that the blogger considers carefully before starting a blog. This is especially important if the blogging is done for the purpose of financial compensation. Ideally, a blog owner should select a blog topic that he or she is passionate about and familiar with. However, bloggers should also carefully consider direct competition as well as the purpose of the blog before starting their blog. This article will discuss these considerations in more detail in an attempt to help bloggers choose a topic for a new blog. This information applies to both bloggers who are completely new to blogging and experienced bloggers who are considering starting a new blog.

Isolating Your Interests

One of the first considerations for a new blogger is his personal interests. This is important because a blogger who is passionate and knowledgeable about a particular topic will not only have an easy time finding ideas for new blog posts, but will also be very successful. This success is likely due to the fact that visitors to the blog can feel their passion for the topic and greatly appreciate informative posts that are informative and accurate.

The blogger's interests can range from topics that are widely popular to topics that are of interest to a small subset of the population. However, there are likely to be interested readers, regardless of the blog's topic. Therefore, bloggers are not discouraged from

choosing to blog on even the most obscure topics. However, bloggers who seek financial gain through high blog traffic should consider selecting a topic that appeals to a broader audience.

Evaluating the Competition

Once a blogger has selected one or more topics he or she is considering for a blog, it is time to start evaluating the competition. This includes looking at other blogs that cover the same topic. This will not only give the blogger a good indication of whether the market is already saturated with blogs on this topic and the quality of existing blogs on this topic. Based on this information, the blogger can make an informed decision about whether or not he or she feels able to compete for blog traffic with existing blogs.

Considering the Purpose of the Blog

Another important consideration for bloggers is the purpose of blogs. Blogs can be created for a variety of reasons, including financial compensation, personal use, or to promote a cause. Bloggers who are starting a blog for personal use may wish to consider their own interests when starting a blog because they are probably not looking for high blog traffic. However, bloggers who create a blog for the purpose of generating profit or promoting a cause need to consider factors such as the ability to generate blog traffic. In these cases, the blogger must choose a topic that will appeal to a large audience. In addition, the Internet should not be saturated with blogs on this topic because it will probably be difficult for the new blog to get a share of the

blog traffic. Finally, blog owners should consider the quality of the blog they are able to create on a particular topic. The blogger should choose a topic that he or she is confident can not only make regular posts, but also ensure that these posts are original, informative and interesting.

Improving your blog's search engine ranking

Bloggers who are interested in reaching a large audience with their blog should consider paying special attention to the search engine optimization of their blog. Reaching a large audience can be a priority for several different reasons. One of the obvious reasons to try to generate more traffic to a blog is to generate revenue. Bloggers who rely on high blog traffic for their revenue are obviously interested in increasing traffic. However, bloggers who create their blog to promote a cause may also be interested in increasing traffic simply to allow their message to reach a wider audience. Regardless of the reason for

74

wanting to increase traffic, one of the best ways to do so is through search engine optimization of the blog. This article will discuss the importance of search engine rankings and offer tips for optimizing a blog.

Why search engine rankings are important

The importance of high search engine rankings is that they can help increase Internet traffic to the blog. This is because Internet users who use search engines to find information on a particular topic are much more likely to visit websites that appear on the first page of search results than to visit websites that appear on later pages of search results. The websites that appear on the first page of the results are likely to get the most traffic. However, Internet users aren't likely to look for more than one or two pages of

search results when looking for more information on a particular topic.

High rankings by search engines essentially act as free advertising for a blog or website. This is because many website users rely on popular search engines to help them find useful information on the Internet. Search engines apply complex algorithms to evaluate websites and rank them according to specific search terms. As a result, Internet users highly value the search results produced and rely on these results to lead them to the best available websites relevant to the keywords they specified in their search.

Tips for Search Engine Optimization

One of the most common ways to optimize a blog or website for search engines is by using relevant keywords. Specifically, the practice of applying specific keyword densities to blog content is a common search engine optimization tactic employed. Blog owners and others trying to optimize their websites do not always agree on the optimal keyword density, but many believe that a percentage of approximately 2% -3% is appropriate.

Another method of optimizing a search engine is to place relevant keywords in the website code. This includes title tags and META tags. This is important because search engines often consider the importance of keywords when evaluating a website. This refers to the location where the keywords

first appear. Placing keywords at the beginning of the website content is useful, but it is important to note that search engines see the code first so that search engines will crawl the keywords that appear before the body of the blog first.

Blog owners can also help increase their search engine rankings by generating backlinks to their blog. This can be accomplished in several different ways. One way to do this is to find other websites willing to place a link to the blog on their website. This is beneficial because many search engines take into account the number of links to a website in their ranking algorithm because these links are considered a website that guarantees the validity of another website. Some website owners may be willing to do this in exchange for a link to their website on their blog. This is known as

a reciprocal link and some search engines may not value this link as much as a non-reciprocal link. There are also some link exchange programs, but these links may not be beneficial because many search engines consider the rank of the website that links to your blog. Therefore, if the website that links to your blog does not rank well, the backlink will not significantly improve search engine rankings.

Blog for everyone?

Blogging is a relatively new phenomenon. It basically involves the creation of an online journal that is displayed in reverse chronological order. The blogger who maintains the blog can choose to post new blog entries as often as he or she wishes. This may involve posting new entries more than once a day, daily, weekly, monthly, or even at a less frequent interval. Blog posts are usually related in some way, but can be about any topic the blogger wants. Bloggers may maintain a blog for a number of different reasons, and these blogs can be private or public in nature. This article will describe the difference between a public and a private blog, and will also explain blogs in a professional way and blogs for personal

reasons.

Private versus public blogs

Blogs can also be private or public. Private Blogs are those where only the blogger and others who have been approved by the blogger can view the blog posts. Public blogs are available to any Internet user. A blogger can choose to make a blog private or public, depending on whether or not he or she feels comfortable having others read the blog. For example, a blogger who creates a blog for the purpose of venting life's frustrations may choose to keep a blog private so that friends or family cannot read these vents. Conversely, a blogger who is blogging for a purpose such as promoting a cause will probably choose to make the blog public so that his or her message reaches as many

Internet users as possible. However, bloggers who create a blog to express themselves through their writing, poetry, or other form of expression may choose to make the blog private or public, depending on whether they want to make these personal feelings available to others. Some bloggers in this situation will make the blog public because they want to reach others who can share their feelings or benefit from reading their blogs. There may be other bloggers in this situation who will make the blog private because they do not want others to see these personal forms of expression.

Blogging professionally

Blogging can actually be done as a source of income for some bloggers. There are several companies that maintain a network of

bloggers and pay bloggers to maintain a blog on the web. These bloggers can be compensated per post, according to the number of visits to the page the blog receives or by a combination of the number of posts and the number of visits to the page. A career as a blogger requires a lot of dedication. The blogger must be willing and able to update the blog regularly and keep the blog interesting to readers.

Blogging for personal reasons

Blogging can also be done for personal reasons. Some bloggers use their blog to keep in touch with family and friends, while others use it to express or share information with others. Blogs created for personal reasons can be a lot of fun, but the blogger should avoid making the process of

maintaining the blog a stressful situation. A blog that is maintained for personal reasons should be an enjoyable experience for the blogger.

Learning about Blogging

There are several different reasons for a blogger to start and maintain a blog. Some of these reasons include generating income, promoting a cause, providing useful information, and keeping in touch with family and friends. Although these reasons for starting a blog can be quite different, all bloggers should spend some time learning about blogs before embarking on a blogging experience. This will help ensure that the blog achieves its intended purpose and will also help prevent the blogger from making mistakes that could be detrimental to a blog. This article will discuss methods for learning about blogging, including studying successful blogs and using the Internet to research blogging. This article will also

briefly explain the importance of promoting a blog.

Studying Successful Blogs

One of the simplest ways for future bloggers and new bloggers to learn about blogs is by studying successful blogs. Those who have recently started a blog or are considering starting a blog can learn a lot simply by reading and studying successful blogs. Bloggers can choose to study blogs that focus on a similar topic, but this is not necessary. Bloggers can learn a lot about how to maintain a successful blog by studying blogs related to any topic. This is because factors such as writing style, blog design, font, and colors can contribute to a blog's success.

When studying other blogs, the blogger should pay special attention to the aspects of the blog that attract his or her attention. This is important because these aspects can also attract other blog visitors and contribute to the success of the blog. Modeling a blog with these aspects in mind can contribute greatly to a blog's success.

Using the Internet to Research Blogging Tips

The Internet can be an excellent resource for learning about blogging. There are a variety of different objects related to this topic. These articles can contain tips for starting, maintaining, and optimizing a blog. They can also contain tips for generating traffic to a blog and keeping visitors interested in the blog. Bloggers are encouraged to carefully

study the information available online and always consider the source of the information. Considering the source of the information is important because it can help ensure that information obtained from the Internet is reliable. However, this can be difficult because it is not always possible to determine the source of information available on the Internet.

Another option for verifying the validity of information available online is to use other sources to confirm the information. This means that a blogger may find an article that provides several tips for operating a successful blog but still search online for information that corroborates the information available in the original article. This may sound redundant, but it can help prevent the blogger from accepting false information as correct.

The importance of promoting a blog

Finally, bloggers should understand the importance of promoting a blog and should investigate methods of promoting their own blog. Promoting a blog is very important because it is through this type of promotion that a blog gains traffic. Gaining traffic is essential to the success of a blog in most cases. The few exceptions include blogs that are maintained solely for the personal use of bloggers, as well as blogs that are maintained for the purpose of keeping friends and family updated on events in the lives of bloggers. All other blogs can benefit from increased blog traffic.

Bloggers can learn about how to successfully

promote a blog by considering how they learned about the blogs they read frequently. This is significant because Internet users who read blogs probably have similar methods of finding these blogs. For example, a blog reader who learned about an interesting blog through participation on a relevant message board will probably consider staying active on message boards that are relevant to his or her own blog as a method of promoting their blog.

Maintaining a successful blog

Creating a blog is relatively simple. However, maintaining a successful blog is a much more difficult process. This is because there are many different factors that can contribute to the success of a blog. Some of these factors include the theme of the blog, the popularity of the blog, and even the aesthetic design of the blog. In addition, the ability to properly promote the blog and reach a large audience of interested Internet users will also have a profound impact on the success of a blog. Although there is no simple formula for creating and maintaining a successful blog, there are some basic tips that can help ensure that a blogger enjoys success

91

with his or her blog. This article will describe some of these basic tips, such as posting new entries regularly, writing for a specific audience, and properly evaluating changes made to the blog.

Posting New Blog Entries Regularly

The importance of posting new blog entries regularly cannot be underestimated. This is very important because periodicals offer dedicated blog visitors an incentive to keep coming back to the blog. Readers may visit a blog originally by chance, but commit to returning to the blog regularly based on the content provided regularly. If the blogger allows the blog to stall, readers have no motivation to keep returning to the blog. However, if there are new posts on a regular basis, it is likely that visitors will return to the

blog often in anticipation of new posts.

The length and depth of a blog post can vary considerably depending on the theme of the blog and the expectations of the target audience. However, in many cases, even a relatively short blog entry that offers only a small amount of information may be enough to keep readers interested. This can be useful when the blogger cannot provide in-depth posts, but in the long run, blog readers seek a certain degree of sustenance and probably expect the blog to be updated with new posts on a regular basis. In addition, they will come to expect a certain voice and quality in the blog posts, so bloggers who enlist the use of guest bloggers should carefully evaluate the guest bloggers to ensure that they are able to post blogs that the audience will appreciate.

Understanding the Blog Audience

Successful bloggers must also be experts in understanding the blog's audience. The most successful blogs focus on a fairly unique niche that attracts a unique set of visitors. By keeping the information posted on the blog related to this niche, the blogger helps ensure that the audience remains interested in the blog. However, the topic is not the only important aspect related to understanding the target audience.

Bloggers also need to be aware of the type of information that blog readers are looking for and how they prefer to be provided with the information. This is important because some blog readers may enjoy long pieces, while others prefer short, to-the-point posts. Even other blog visitors may prefer that posts be

provided as bullet points in an easy to read manner. Providing the information in a way that visitors can easily process the information is as important as providing quality information.

Evaluating changes to the blog

Finally, all successful bloggers know how to make changes to the blog carefully and evaluate the effects these changes have on the blog's traffic. This is critical because an already successful blog can be doomed to failure if the blogger makes an opportunity that is not appreciated by dedicated visitors and does not address the concerns of the readers. To avoid this potential problem, bloggers should be careful to make only one change at a time and allow enough time to evaluate the effect the change has on website

traffic, as well as the readers' comments before deciding whether to reverse the change or make additional changes.

Similarly, a blog that seeks to increase website traffic may have problems if it makes too many changes and does not evaluate how these changes are affecting the blog's traffic. A better strategy would be to make small changes one at a time and evaluate the effect of the change carefully before making more changes. This will help guide the blogger to produce a successful blog.

Manage multiple blogs

While some bloggers may focus exclusively on one blog at a time, there are many bloggers who manage to maintain several different blogs at the same time. However, not all bloggers do this successfully. Some bloggers compromise both the quality of content and the quantity of content by trying to maintain too many blogs, while other bloggers have the ability to keep several blogs updated and interesting to visitors. There are some key elements to maintaining multiple successful blogs. This article will discuss some of these elements, including maintaining original content, keeping blogs updated, and budgeting time to work on each blog.

Maintaining Original Content

Bloggers who maintain multiple blogs should be careful to maintain the content of each original blog. Even if the blogger maintains several related blogs, it is important to ensure that each of these blogs has original blog posts. This will help prevent blog visitors from feeling that the information they receive is not original. It will also help prevent readers who frequently visit one or more of the bloggers' blogs from deciding to start visiting only one of the blogs because they feel the posts are redundant.

Bloggers are also advised not to steal posts from other similar blogs. Not only is this illegal, but it is also unlikely to help the

blogger much because dedicated readers of the original blog are likely to realize that the new blog is simply stealing content from a more successful blog.

Keeping Each Blog Up-to-Date

Bloggers who maintain multiple blogs are also advised to ensure that each blog is kept up to date. This means that they should take care to post to each blog regularly. Doing this will help avoid problems arising from visitors to the blog feeling that the blogs are stagnant. Even the most interesting and informative blogs can quickly lose traffic if blog visitors do not see new content on a regular basis. The Internet is constantly evolving and updating. As a result, Internet users can afford to be picky and are unlikely to stay engaged with a blog that does not

publish new information regularly because they are likely to find other blogs available that provide more frequent updates.

Finding time to work on each blog

Bloggers who maintain several blogs also have the task of finding time to work on each blog. However, this is very important because bloggers cannot afford to neglect one or more of their blogs. Doing this can result in a marked decrease in blog traffic. Therefore, bloggers who want to maintain several blogs should budget their time carefully to ensure that they spend enough time on each blog. This time management exercise can begin by assessing the needs of each blog. Some blogs may require a large amount of time and effort each week to keep the blog running smoothly, while other blogs

may require only a small amount of time for the same purpose. In general, blogs that require a large amount of research will require more blogger time and energy than blogs that are based on the opinions and feelings of the bloggers and therefore do not require as much research. Once the blogger has determined how long it will take to maintain each blog, he or she can schedule their time accordingly. However, he or she should plan to evaluate how well each blog is working and may need to make adjustments to the schedule as needed. In addition, you may need to make a decision to delete a blog or request assistance in keeping the blogs updated if necessary.

Supervising your child's blog

Blogs are becoming increasingly popular and this popularity is not just among adults. Young children are also becoming interested in blogs. With the advent of social networking sites such as MySpace, blogs are growing by leaps and bounds. Internet users now have a variety of options available to them for publishing and maintaining a blog. In addition, the growing popularity of blogs currently available promotes interest in blogging with other Internet users. Children are bombarded daily with a variety of blogs available online and are understandably interested in creating blogs of their own. In most cases, children create blogs for social

reasons, but there are some smart kids who realize the profit potential of blogs. While there are a lot of benefits kids can get from blogging, there are also some risks involved. Therefore, parents should carefully monitor their children's blog, as well as all their Internet use. This article will discuss the issue of monitoring a child's blog in more detail.

Discuss blog expectations with children

The first step parents should take when a child is interested in creating a blog is to thoroughly discuss expectations with the child. The child and the parents should have an open and honest discussion about responsible Internet use. This is important because these conversations can lay the foundation for how the child will behave online. There are certain dangers on the

Internet, but parents who understand these dangers and communicate with their children to share this potential for danger, as well as information on how to stay safe while online, are likely to have children who stay safe while online.

When a child is considering starting a blog, the parent should be involved in the process from the beginning. The parent should not only be aware of the child's intention to start blogging, but also be aware of the child's reason for wanting to blog and intentions for the blog. This is important because it can help parents establish appropriate guidelines for blogging. For example, a child may be interested in social networking through blogging, but should understand that there is the potential for danger with this type of blogging. Parents should limit the content of the blog and should advise children to avoid

revealing personal information such as their full name, address, and phone number on the blog. Other information that could be used to identify and locate the child should also be avoided.

Periodically review your child's blog

In addition to discussing blogs with the child and establishing ground rules for blog content, parents should also regularly visit the blog to make sure that the established rules are being followed. Parents should review their child's blogs on a regular basis, but should not inform them when these reviews will take place. This will help prevent children from altering the blog to remove questionable material during the review and to replace this material once the review is complete. This is important because

it would be fairly simple for the child to make changes quickly simply by saving files and replacing them with appropriate blog posts during scheduled reviews.

Monitoring the blogs your child frequents

Parents should also consider regularly monitoring the blogs their children frequent. This is important because the information children see online can be harmful to children. It is also important because most blogs provide visitors with the opportunity to communicate with the blogger. In most cases, this communication is in the form of comments left for the blogger, and the blogger can choose to respond to these comments. In some cases, the visitor may even have the opportunity to provide personal contact information to the blogger.

Parents who remain aware of the blogs their children visit can review these blogs carefully to ensure that their children do not behave inappropriately online and do not accidentally take risks with the actions they take.

 EXPERT BLOGGER

Optimizing your blog for search engines

Bloggers who are interested in generating a lot of traffic to their blog and maintaining a successful blog should pay special attention to search engine optimization techniques that can help improve the search engine rankings of their blogs. All search engines employ some sort of ranking algorithm that is used to determine the order in which websites are returned when an Internet user searches for information on a particular topic. However, not all search engines use the same algorithm for this purpose. As a result, there is no simple solution for optimizing a blog for high rankings in all search engines. However, there are some tips that can be useful with

most search engines. These tips include using relevant keywords, generating links to your blogs and using image tags in a beneficial way.

The importance of keywords

Using relevant keywords in blog posts is one of the most common ways and also one of the simplest ways to optimize search engine rankings. However, not all bloggers agree on the best ways to use relevant keywords to optimize search engine rankings. Some bloggers believe that keywords should often be used to create high keyword densities, while others believe that using keywords in densities lower than 1% -3% and paying attention to keyword placement is the most valuable strategy. Other bloggers argue that simply using relevant keywords, since they

come naturally in the flow of blog posts, is enough to ensure that search engines understand the blog content.

Regardless of the keyword strategy, a blogger who chooses to employ all bloggers can benefit from researching relevant keywords. They may have a blog that refers to a general topic, such as gardening, but may not know the search terms that Internet user typically use when researching this topic. Fortunately, there are many programs available that generate related keywords for a particular time, giving the blogger other keywords that they should consider incorporating into the blog. For the example of a blog related to gardening, the blogger can use additional keywords such as container gardening or home gardening to attract more interest from search engine users.

Generating Favorable Back Links

Backlinks are also another common factor used in search engine ranking algorithms. Many search engines consider the amount of links pointing to a website, as well as the quality of the websites providing these links. This means that the search engine rankings of the website pointing to your blog could influence the amount of weight that the backlink contributes to their own rankings. This is because some search engines consider higher ranking websites to be more valuable than other websites that do not rank well, and therefore favorably reward websites that link to these high ranking websites.

Some search engine algorithms also consider

whether backlinks are reciprocal or non-reciprocal. In these cases, non-reciprocal links are generally considered more valuable than reciprocal links. In addition, backlinks that come from link exchanges or link farms are generally not considered very influential in search engine rankings.

How images can improve search engine rankings

Bloggers should also be aware that any images used on their blog can be used to improve search engine rankings with some search engines. This aspect of search engine optimization is often overlooked because many bloggers believe that images are not seen by search engines. While this is true, search engines crawl the blog code in addition to the blog content. This means that

the search engine will see the information provided in the image tags. Bloggers can leverage this by using image tags to provide relevant keywords that can boost search engine rankings. However, care should be taken to ensure that the keywords used in these tags also accurately describe the image because blog visitors will often see the text included in these tags when they scroll over an image on the blog.

Ordering when you buy online

Online shoppers have a variety of options available for placing an order. Online shopping is already quite convenient for several reasons, including the convenience and ability to purchase items from retailers around the world. The ability to order in a variety of different ways makes online shopping more desirable for some consumers. This article will discuss some of the options available for placing an order when shopping online, including using the website to place the order, calling customer service to place the order, and faxing or mailing.

 EXPERT BLOGGER

Ordering through the website

One of the most popular options for ordering when you shop online is to order directly through the online retailer's website. In most cases, online retailers offer the ability to add items to a virtual shopping cart while browsing the available items being offered for sale. After the consumer has finished shopping, they can review the contents of their shopping cart and add, subtract or modify the shopping cart contents as necessary before continuing with the checkout process of the online shopping experience. During the checkout process, the consumer provides information such as credit card information and billing address, as well as the address to which they would like to ship the items. The online shopper can choose to have the item shipped to themselves or others. While online purchases

are generally considered secure, consumers should verify that the website is on a secure server that will protect confidential information. One way to do this is to look at the website address. Secure websites begin with https: // while non-secure websites begin with http: //.

Calling Customer Service to place an order

Online shoppers can search for items online, but may decide to purchase them by calling a customer service representative instead of ordering online. Customers may choose this option for several different reasons. Some online retailers may not have an option to complete the purchase online or these features may not work properly, and in these cases the buyer will probably order by phone. However, there are situations where a

consumer may choose to call customer service to place an order, even when it is possible to do so online. This may include situations where the order is particularly complex or situations where the consumer has questions that he or she would like answered before placing an order. Online shoppers who make a purchase in this manner should have all necessary information available before contacting customer service. This information includes product number, billing information and shipping information.

Fax or mail shipments

Online shoppers can also fax or mail order to the online retailer. The consumer can search for items online and even print the order form from the online retailer's website.

Although this is not the most common method of online shopping, there are some consumers who still use this method. One example of using this method is the ability to pay for an order with a check instead of a credit card. A credit card may be required for orders placed online or with a customer service representative. Customers who fax or mail an order form may have the option of using a credit card to pay for the order, but may also have the option of using a check. This is ideal for online shoppers who do not have a credit card or do not want to charge items to a credit card. While there are some advantages to this method of ordering from an online retailer, there is one major disadvantage to this method. This disadvantage is that the order may take longer to process than it would with other methods. When a customer places an order through a website or by phone, the order is usually processed instantly. However, when

the consumer submits the order form, it may take a few days to arrive and then may require additional time for processing. Even orders that are faxed may not be processed immediately despite arriving quickly.

Products to facilitate blogs

There are a variety of products that can simplify the blogging process. Although blogging is not a difficult process, there may be some aspects of blogging that are overwhelming to new bloggers or bloggers who do not have much experience on the Internet. These products can be very beneficial to the blogger by simplifying the design process or helping to make the blog more appealing to the readers of the blog. This article will discuss some of the products currently available to facilitate blogging, including blogging software programs, website design software, and keyword generators.

Blogging software programs

Blogging software programs are some of the most obvious programs that make blogging easy. These programs are readily available and many of them are free to use. Blogging software programs can greatly simplify the process of publishing a blog, especially if the blogger uses the templates included in these programs. In some cases, the act of publishing a blog once the blog has been set up can be as simple as writing the blog text in a text editor and pressing a button to publish the blog. However, it will require some advance work by the blogger to set up the blog layout.

Even the layout process is greatly simplified with these programs, especially if the blogger chooses to use the templates in the program.

The blogger may simply have to scroll through a list of options and select the ones that seem most appealing to him or her. Based on these selections, the software will generate the blog with the appropriate layout, colors, fonts, and even advertising options. More ambitious bloggers may choose to use their programming skills to customize these templates, but this is not necessary and the blog will work well enough without any additional customization.

Website design software

Website design software can also be a useful tool for new bloggers who want to create a blog that is aesthetically appealing and functional. These software programs make it possible for bloggers who have no design

experience to create a blog with a unique look. Using this type of software, the blogger can scroll through options, make changes on the fly, preview changes, and even upload photos to use in the blog. As these changes are made in the software design program, the code for these design options is automatically generated, updated, and stored as needed.

Keyword generators

Bloggers trying to attract a large amount of web traffic to a website should also consider using the keyword generator to help them determine which keywords they should use on their blog. The blogger may want the blog to be interesting and informative as a priority, but judicious use of keywords throughout the blog and in the blog code can contribute to higher search engine rankings

for the blog. This is important because high search engine rankings often translate into high blog traffic. This is because Internet users rely heavily on search engines to help them find the best websites belonging to certain keywords that are used during searches. These high search engine rankings essentially act as free advertising for the blog owner because Internet users expect higher ranking websites to be the most informative websites, so they are likely to visit blogs that rank well with search engines rather than blogs that are buried further down the search result pages.⏎

Promoting your blog

Blogging can be a lot of fun for some bloggers, but for others it's a source of income. Whether this revenue is earned through an AdSense campaign, paid ads, affiliate marketing or some other type of revenue source, one of the key elements to maximizing this benefit is driving more traffic to the blog. This is because the more visitors the blog receives, the more opportunities there are for the blogger to get visitors to click on the blog ads. There are some basic techniques that bloggers can rely on to promote their blog and increase traffic to their blog. This article will cover some of these key concepts, including participating in relevant message boards, optimizing the blog for search engines, and keeping the blog

interesting for visitors.

Active participation in message boards

Posting on message boards that relate to the blog's topic is actually a very simple way for blog owners to direct traffic to their blog. However, a warning to use this type of promotion for the blog is to avoid violating the rules of the message board. This is important because some message boards have strict regulations regarding the inclusion of links to other websites on the message board. Failure to comply with these guidelines may result in the blogger being kicked off the message board and may also cause other message board users to think less of the blog owner.

Another careful consideration for the blog owner is to avoid posting the web address on his or her blog in a way that will be considered spam by other message board users. This is important because other message board users are unlikely to visit the blog if they think the blog owner is simply spamming the message board. This can be avoided by including the link to the blog in the signature and by ensuring that posts made to the message board are informative and of interest to other message board users. Building a reputation as a useful contributor to the message board will be beneficial in attracting other message board users to visit the blog.

Optimizing your blog

Search engine optimization is another factor

that blog owners should also carefully consider. Search engine optimization of the blog can be beneficial because improved search engine rankings often lead to increased blog traffic. Depending on the amount of competition on the blog topic, climbing to the top of search engine rankings is not always easy. Blog owners who have a blog with a popular theme may face strong competition for search engine rankings from other blogs and websites that may have the means to hire professionals in the search engine optimization industry to help them achieve high rankings. However, there are some steps that the blogger can take to try to raise the rankings. Some of these steps include researching and using naturally relevant keywords throughout the blog posts, incorporating these keywords into the title, META and image tags and avoiding black hat optimization techniques that could result in the blog being penalized by search

engines.

Keeping your blog interesting

Finally, one of the simplest ways a blog owner can help drive traffic to his or her blog is by regularly updating the blog and keeping it interesting. This is important because a blog that is interesting is much more likely to not only keep the blog traffic but also generate new traffic. This is because readers interested in blog posts are likely to not only keep coming back to the blog, but also recommend it to other members of the target audience. This type of word-of-mouth advertising can be very beneficial because those who have an interest in the content of a particular blog often also have friends who would also be interested in the blog. Once a blog owner recommends a blog to one or

more friends, it is likely that these new blog visitors will also recommend it to others if they find it interesting, useful or otherwise worthwhile.

Tips to keep your blog up to date

Keeping a blog up-to-date is one of the most important aspects of blogging. This is very important because regular visitors to the blog expect new posts on a regular basis. Not all visitors expect to see a new post as often as once a day, but most blog readers expect the blog content to be updated regularly. In most cases, visitors expect new content at least weekly. However, depending on the topic, visitors may expect updates on a more frequent basis. Similarly, visitors may not be interested in receiving this type of information more than a few times a year. Blog owners should be aware of the frequency with which readers expect new

posts and should make an effort to compel readers with updates as often. This article will discuss methods for keeping a blog updated, including scheduling a regular schedule for blogging, using publishing tools wisely, and hiring guest bloggers when necessary.

Finding Time to Publish Daily

One way to help ensure that a blog stays current is to schedule a daily blog posting schedule. This is especially important when blog readers expect new posts daily or at least several times a week. Bloggers who allocate a specific block of time each day to research, write, and post blogs are more likely to have an up-to-date blog than bloggers who plan to complete tasks when they find time to do so. There may still be

days when the blogger can't post a new blog post, but these days will be less frequent than if the blogger doesn't have a block of time strictly dedicated to keeping the blog up to date.

On days when the blogger can't spend time blogging, the blogger may want to at least post a brief message explaining why a new blog entry was not possible. This will let readers know that you are aware of their desire to read more information, but simply cannot post a new blog entry. Until this becomes commonplace, it is unlikely that visitors to the blog will stop seeing a blog simply because the blogger skips a day or two.

Taking advantage of publishing tools

Some blog publishing tools allow bloggers to write blog posts in advance and specify when each post should be published. This is a great feature for bloggers who want to post new entries daily but can't make time each day to write blog entries. This way, the blogger can spend a block of time each week writing blog posts and posting them throughout the week. This is often an easier method for many bloggers because they can be more efficient this way.

Hiring guest bloggers

Bloggers may also consider hiring guest bloggers to help them keep a blog up to date. This can be a valuable method for bloggers

who not only have difficulty keeping their blog up to date, but are also interested in providing readers with a little variety. However, blog owners who choose this approach to keeping their blog up to date should carefully consider how dedicated readers will react to this change. This is important because some readers may not be interested in reading blogs written by a guest blogger. Therefore, using a guest blogger may be more detrimental to the blog than not updating it regularly. Bloggers can measure readers' reaction to the use of guest bloggers in two different ways. The simplest and most direct method is to survey readers about their use of guest bloggers. This can be done by asking readers to comment on the topic and tabulating the comments received. Another method of measuring reader reaction is to introduce a guest blogger and compare the traffic the guest blogger receives to the traffic the blog owner receives.

Use of guest bloggers

Owners of a successful blog that has many followers may sometimes have the need to use guest bloggers. An example of when this practice might be a good idea is when the owner of a popular blog will not be available to post new blog entries for an extended period of time. In this case, the lack of blog updates can cause the blog to lose traffic, so it would be prudent for the blog owner to arrange for a guest blogger or a number of guest bloggers to post new articles during his or her absence. The blogger may also announce the intention to use guest bloggers during this time period to ensure that loyal visitors to the blog are aware of the situation and that it is only temporary. This article will discuss aspects of using guest bloggers,

136

including advertising guest bloggers, selecting guest bloggers, and compensating guest bloggers.

Advertising for guest bloggers

There are several places where a blog owner can advertise for guest bloggers. Job boards specifically for bloggers or freelance writers are an excellent option for finding guest bloggers. Blogger job boards are frequently visited by experienced bloggers looking for new opportunities to blog for compensation. These bloggers may have specific experience with the topic of the blog or may simply be experts in creating interesting blogs on a variety of topics. Job boards for freelance writers are another great option. These writers may not necessarily have blogging experience, but they may have other writing

experience that is useful. Blog owners should consider posting a detailed message that specifies the type of work required and the length of the project and ask for clips of the writers that can be used to check the writer's skill level.

Blog owners may also wish to advertise for guest bloggers on message boards related to the blog topic. Visitors to this blog may not necessarily have writing experience, but they are likely to be quite knowledgeable about the blog topic and therefore able to produce interesting and insightful blogs.

Selection of guest bloggers

The selection of a guest blogger should be done with care to ensure that the guest

blogger is reliable and capable of producing articulate, informative, and interesting blog posts. Blog owners who advertise for a guest blogger on the blogger and freelance job boards should request clips that demonstrate the writer's ability to write blogs that are interesting and informative. When advertising on a message board for a guest blogger, the blog owner may consider using the applicant's previous postings to assess his or her writing ability and knowledge of the topic. He or she should also consider the type of response that the applicant's message board postings typically elicit. This is important because it is a good indication of the type of response that blogs will generate. Blog owners should also ask applicants for references and should contact these references for information about the bloggers' work ethic and ability to complete projects.

Guest Blogger Compensation

Blog owners should also carefully consider how they intend to compensate guest bloggers. This can be done in the form of financial compensation or by allowing the guest blogger to post a short biography with a link to their website or personal blog at the end of the blog posting. The latter form of compensation is essentially free advertising space for the guest blogger. The blog owner may also wish to compensate the guest blogger with a combination of money and free advertising space. Regardless of the method of compensation chosen, the blog owner should discuss this with the guest blogger before starting the work and should sign a written contract with the guest blogger that explicitly states the terms of the compensation to avoid disputes.

When others don't approve of your blog

Regardless of the topic of a blog, all bloggers face the potential of situations where others do not approve of their blog. While this type of reaction is popular among blogs focused on political or controversial issues, bloggers who maintain a personal blog may also face disapproval from those who do not approve of bloggers' choices in life. This article will discuss issues such as dealing with negative comments on a blog, dealing with criticism from friends and family, and addressing situations where blogs can cause legal problems for the blogger.

Dealing with negative comments on your blog

Negative comments posted on a blog are one of the most common forms of disapproval that a blog can receive. These comments can be posted in response to a specific blog post or they can be posted as an objection to the blog in general. These negative comments can be very upsetting to the blogger, but fortunately there are some methods for dealing with these comments.

Bloggers who are concerned that negative comments may influence other readers of the blog have some options for dealing with these negative comments. One way to do this is to set up the blog to not allow comments. This will effectively remove the comments, but it will also remove the comments from

the blog's supporters. Another option a blogger has is to simply remove negative comments as they are found. This is not a very effective method because other readers may have time to read the comments before they are removed. Bloggers who are online often and are not concerned about negative comments appearing on the blog for a short period of time can use this method. Another method of dealing with negative comments includes refuting these comments on the blog. Finally, bloggers often have the opportunity to prohibit visitors who leave negative comments from making future comments.

Dealing with criticism from friends and family

Bloggers can also be criticized by friends and

family for the content of their blogs. Friends and family cannot use the comments section to express their disapproval, but they can express their concerns directly to the blogger in person, by phone, or by email. This can be a difficult situation for bloggers because they may be torn between keeping the blog in line with their vision and keeping their friends and family happy. In many cases, friends and family members may object to a blog because they believe it may be potentially harmful to the blogger or because they are concerned about how the blog will reflect on them. In these sensitive situations, the blogger has the option of removing or modifying the blog or talking to friends and family to explain their feelings without making changes to the blog.

When Blogs Can Cause Legal Problems

Bloggers should be aware that there are some situations in which their blog may cause legal problems. Making statements about another person that are false and defamatory may cause the blog topic to seek retaliation for defamation. Other blog postings may also be found to be illegal for a wide variety of other reasons. Bloggers may assume that freedom of speech laws fully protect them, but there may be situations where statements on a blog are not protected by freedom of speech laws and the blogger faces legal ramifications for his or her posts. Blogs that violate someone else's copyright laws can also cause legal problems.

Succeed in your venture and become an EXPERT BLOGGER!

 EXPERT BLOGGER

Visit our author page on Amazon and get more MENTES LIBRES!

http://amazon.com/author/menteslibres

If you wish, you can leave a comment on this book by clicking on the following link so that we can continue to grow! Thank you very much for your purchase!

https://www.amazon.com/dp/B0839NGN55

www.ingramcontent.com/pod-product-compliance
Lightning Source LLC
Chambersburg PA
CBHW071137050326

40690CB00008B/1488